Thank you for purchasing the first ever Calen*draw*™!

Your Boston-themed 2016 Coloring Book Calendar includes twelve (12) illustrations of significant, well-loved places in and around the city, illustrated by former Massachusetts College of Art student and life-long Massachusetts resident, Jillsy Taylor.

Choose your favorite colored pencils, crayons, or markers, turn off your phone, try to limit other distractions, and calm your mind as you draw and color the city of Boston to life. You can color each month one at a time, as you turn the pages, or color them all ahead of time - one thing is certain; your unique artwork will be on display, year-round, while you stay organized!

List of Included Illustrations:

January	"The T" passing by "The Garden"
February	The dinosaur who welcomes guests to the Museum of Science
March	The Public Garden's famous ducklings
April	The Marathon finish line
May	The Public Garden bridge
June	The amazing entrance to Chinatown
July	The Esplanade's Hatch Shell
August	The Kenmore Square sign we all know and love
September	A beautiful cobblestone street in the North End
October	Fenway: "America's Most Beloved Ballpark"
November	The Mayflower II
December	The statue of famous rider and silversmith, Paul Revere

Share your favorite pages (and check out how others have colored theirs) on social media with the hashtag **#Calendraw**!

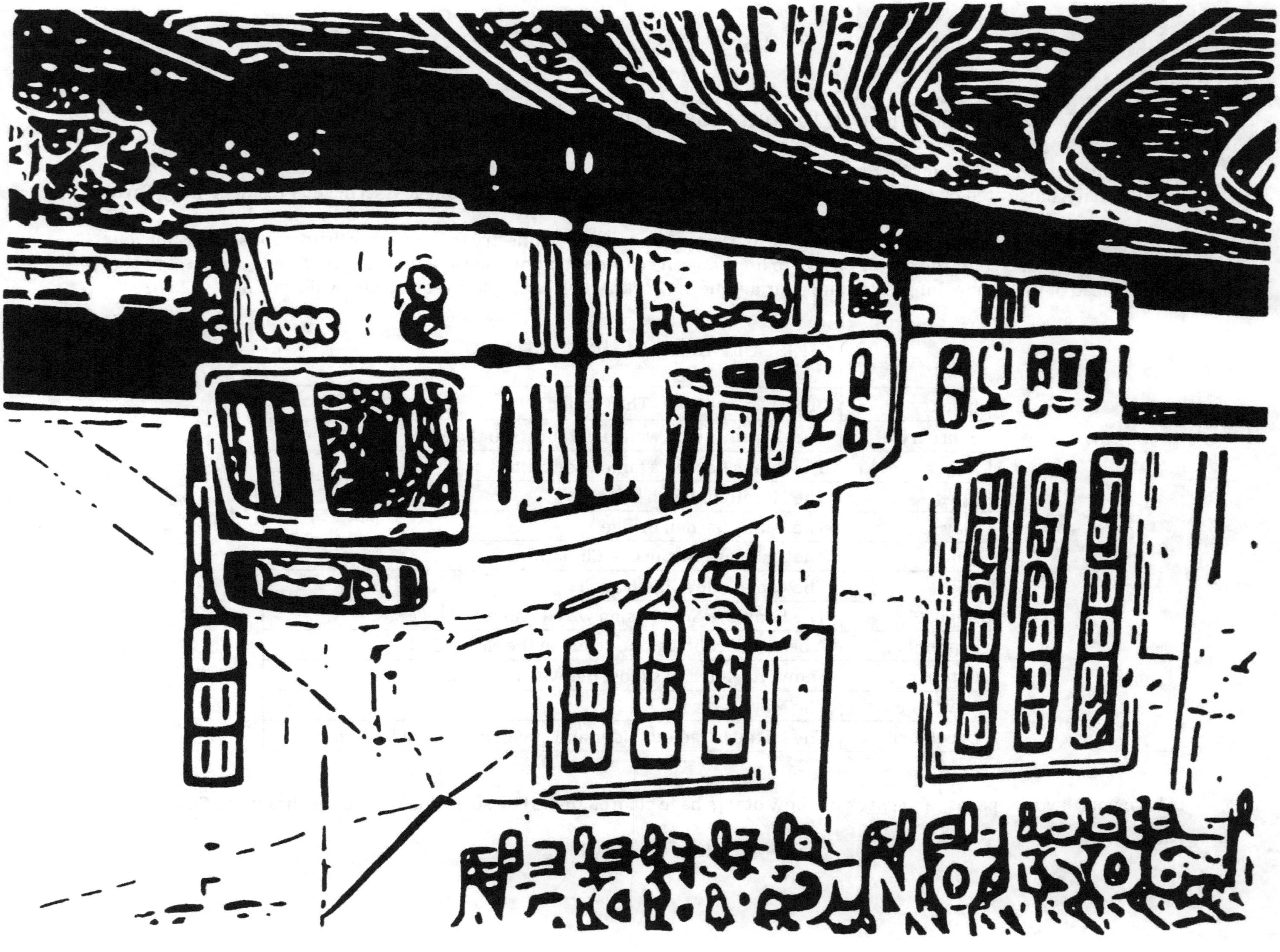

JANUARY 2016

Sunday	Monday	Tuesday	Wednesday	Thursday	Friday	Saturday
					1	2
3	4	5	6	7	8	9
10	11	12	13	14	15	16
17	18	19	20	21	22	23
24	25	26	27	28	29	30
31	Notes:					

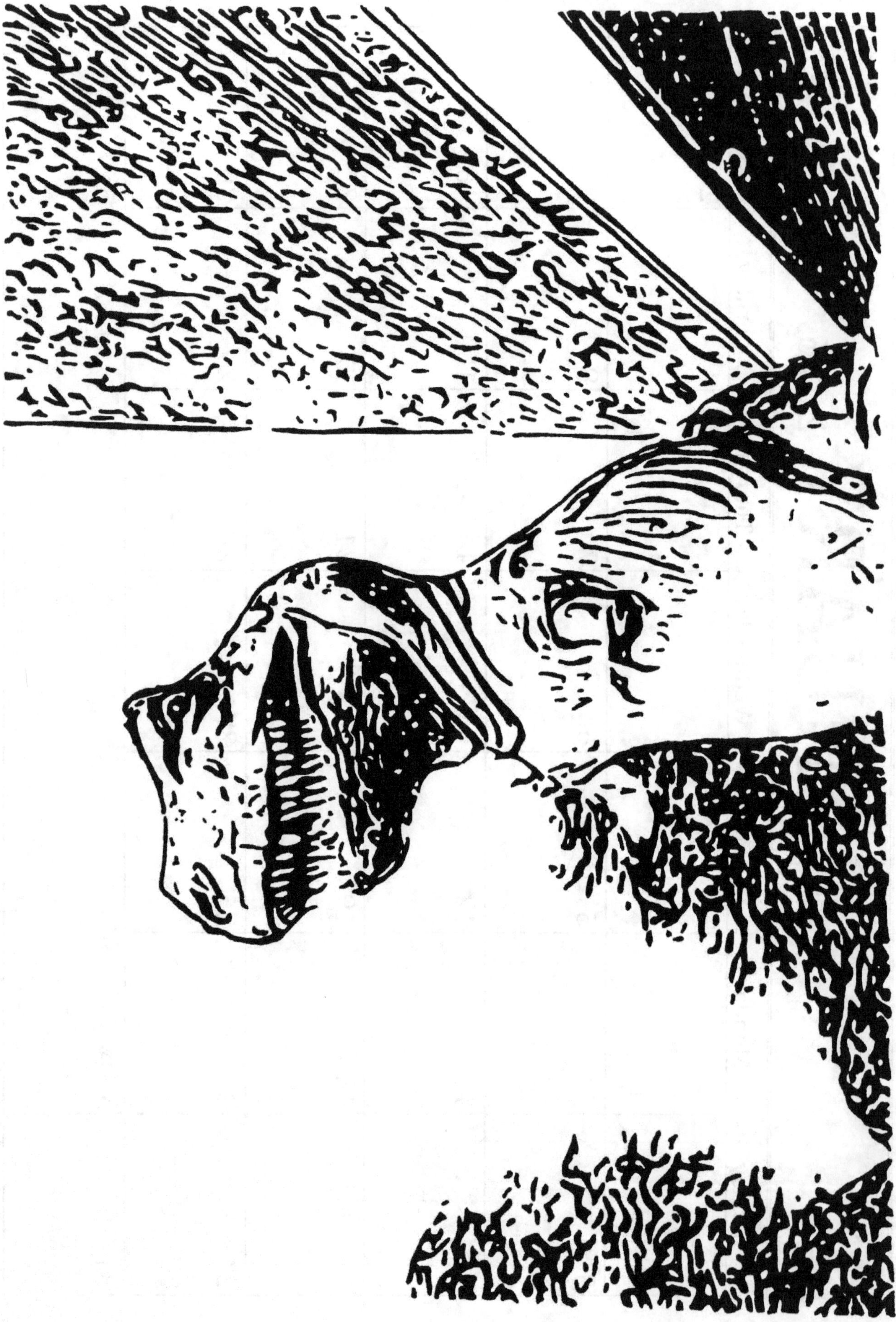

FEBRUARY 2016

Sunday	Monday	Tuesday	Wednesday	Thursday	Friday	Saturday
	1	2	3	4	5	6
7	8	9	10	11	12	13
14	15	16	17	18	19	20
21	22	23	24	25	26	27
28	29					

Notes:

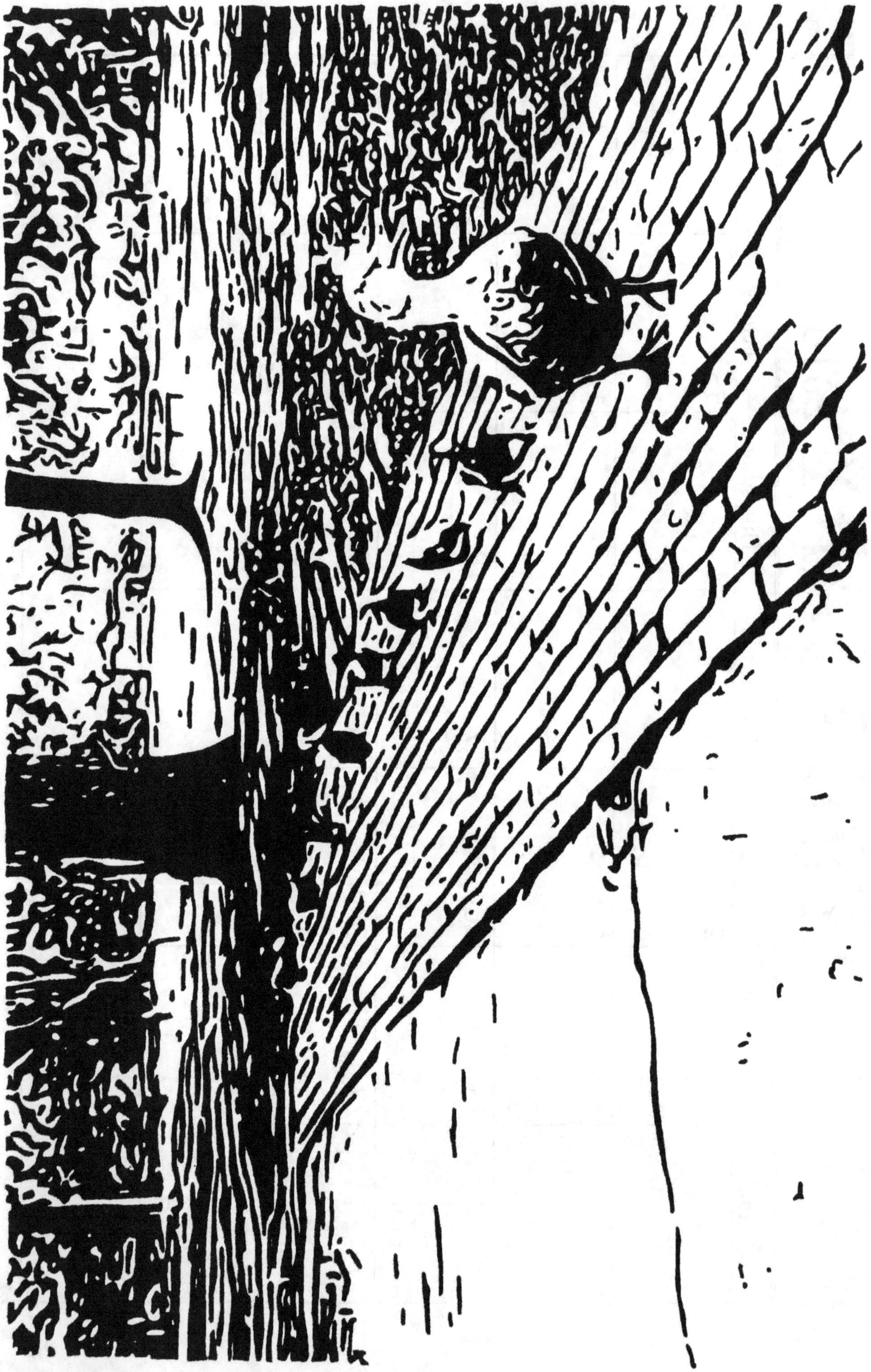

MARCH 2016

Sunday	Monday	Tuesday	Wednesday	Thursday	Friday	Saturday
		1	2	3	4	5
6	7	8	9	10	11	12
13	14	15	16	17	18	19
20	21	22	23	24	25	26
27	28	29	30	31		

Notes:

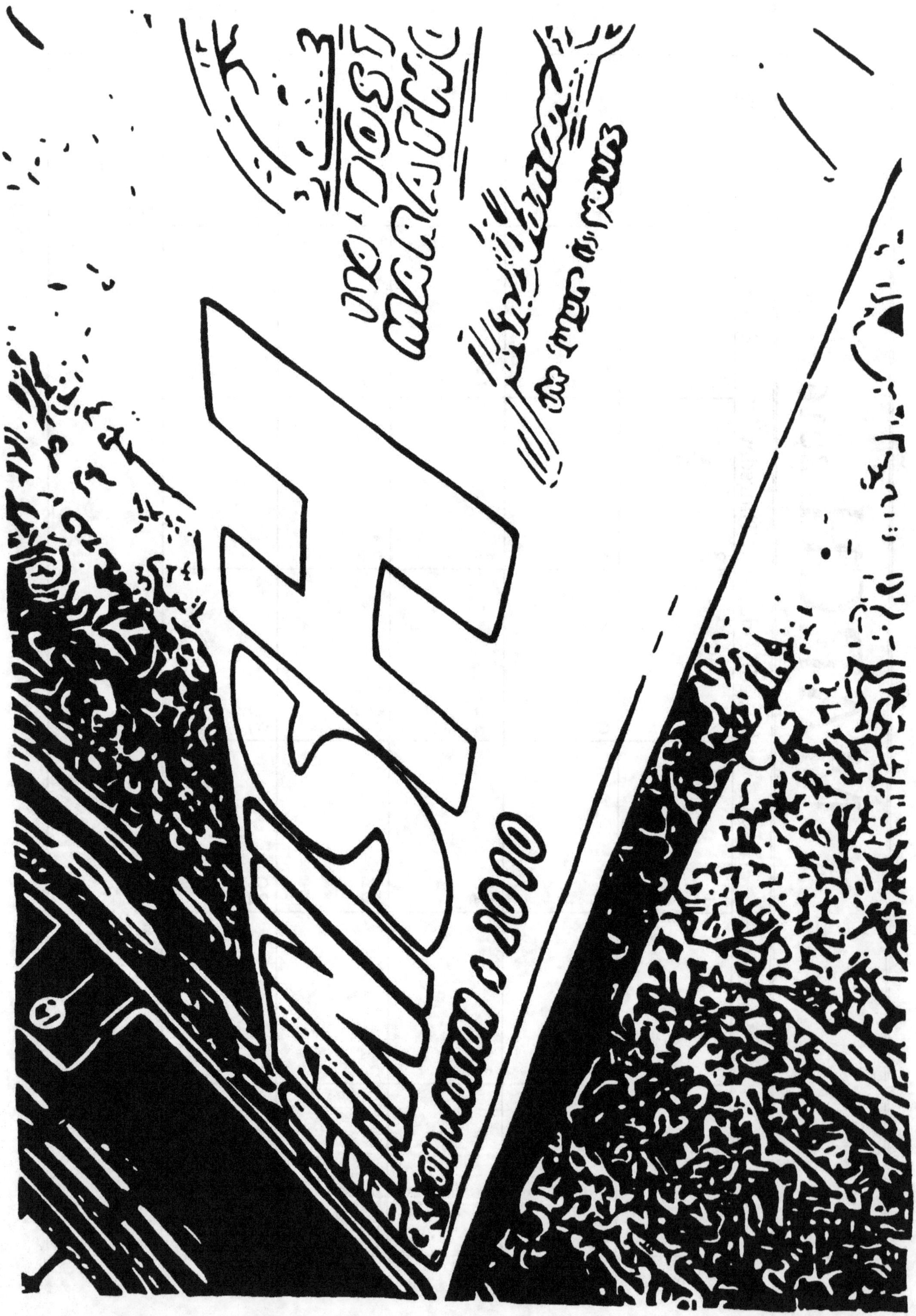
VHS

APRIL 2016

Sunday	Monday	Tuesday	Wednesday	Thursday	Friday	Saturday
					1	2
3	4	5	6	7	8	9
10	11	12	13	14	15	16
17	18	19	20	21	22	23
24	25	26	27	28	29	30

Notes:

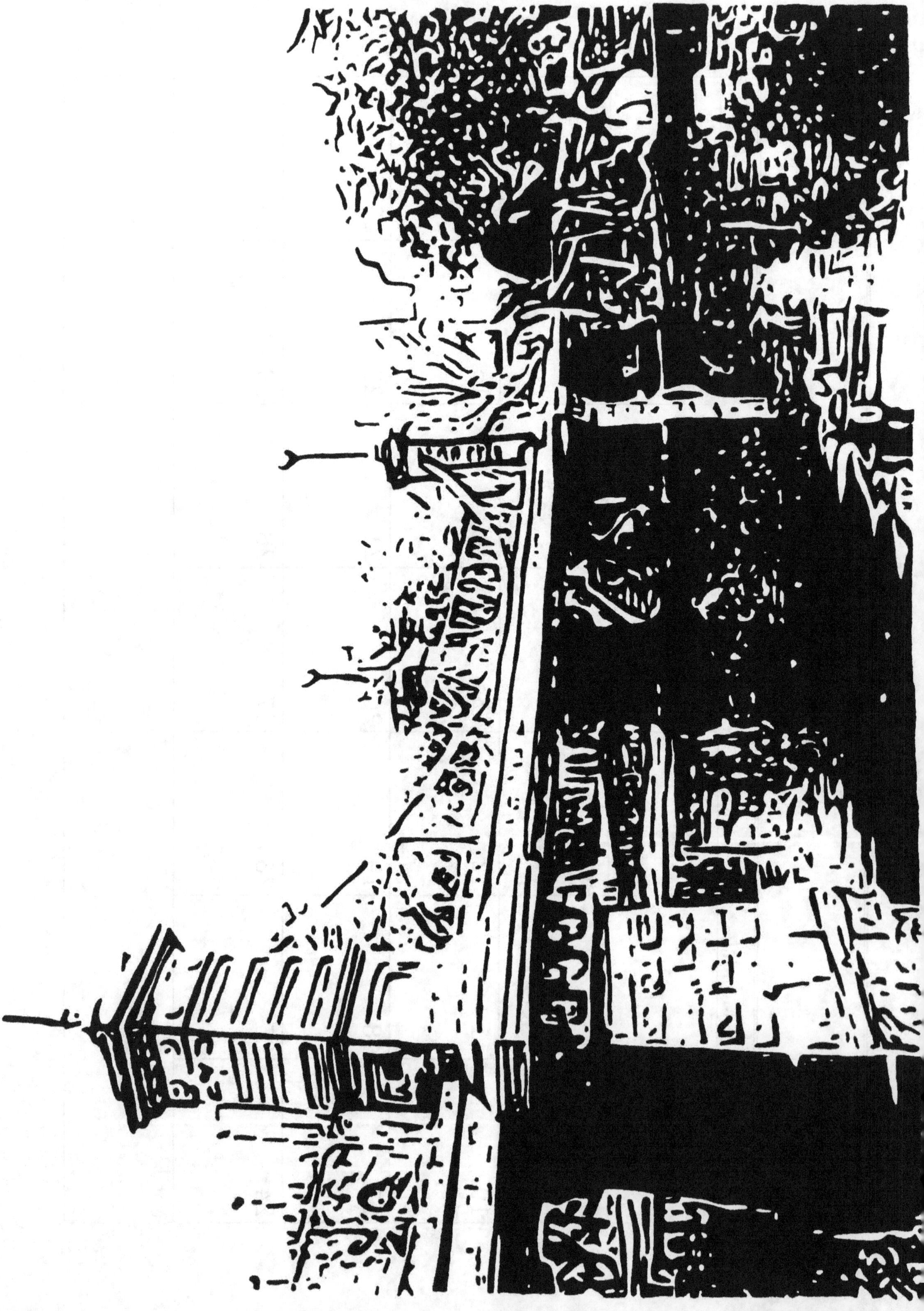

MAY 2016

Sunday	Monday	Tuesday	Wednesday	Thursday	Friday	Saturday
1	2	3	4	5	6	7
8	9	10	11	12	13	14
15	16	17	18	19	20	21
22	23	24	25	26	27	28
29	30	31				

Notes:

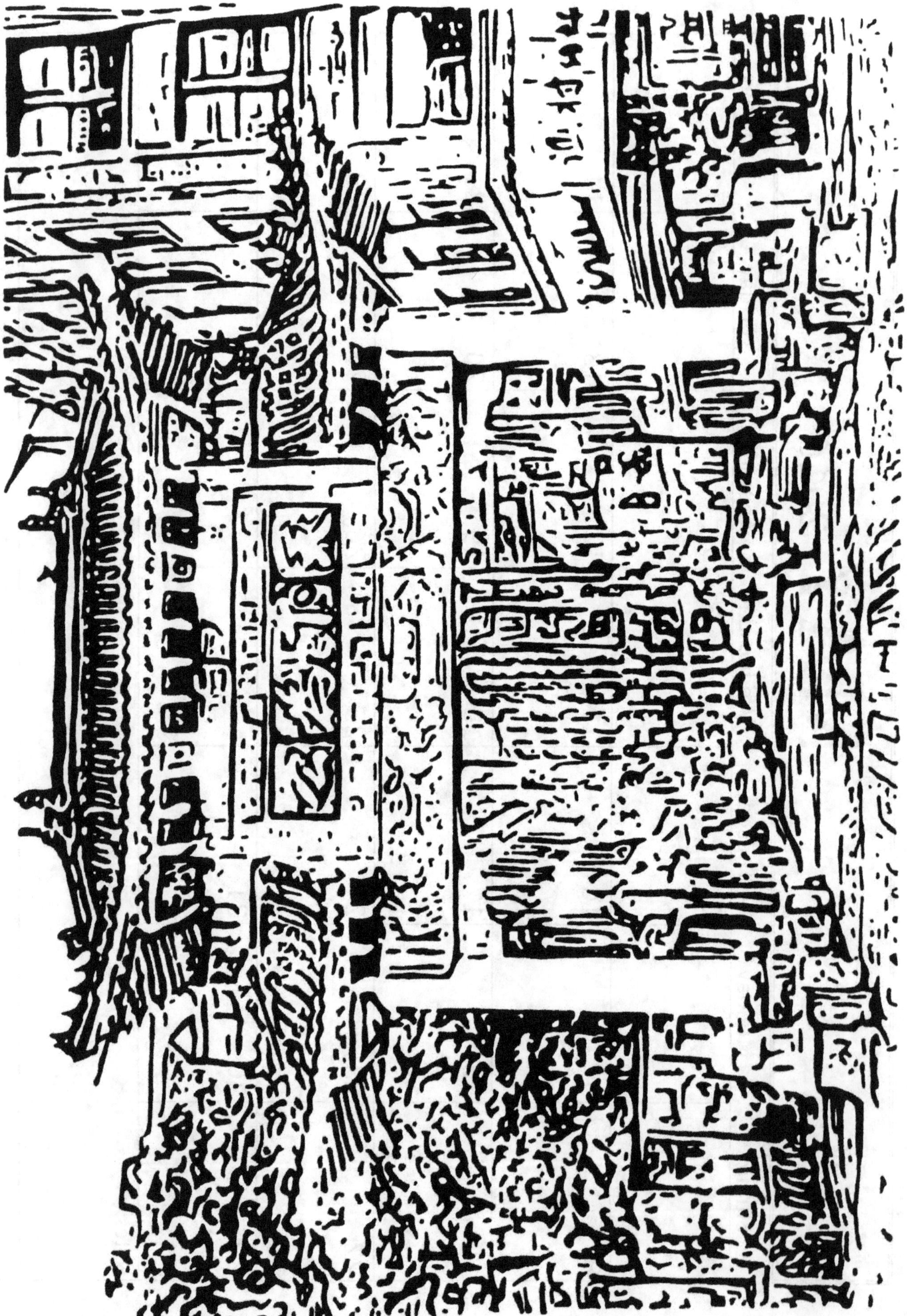

JUNE 2016

Sunday	Monday	Tuesday	Wednesday	Thursday	Friday	Saturday
			1	2	3	4
5	6	7	8	9	10	11
12	13	14	15	16	17	18
19	20	21	22	23	24	25
26	27	28	29	30		

Notes:

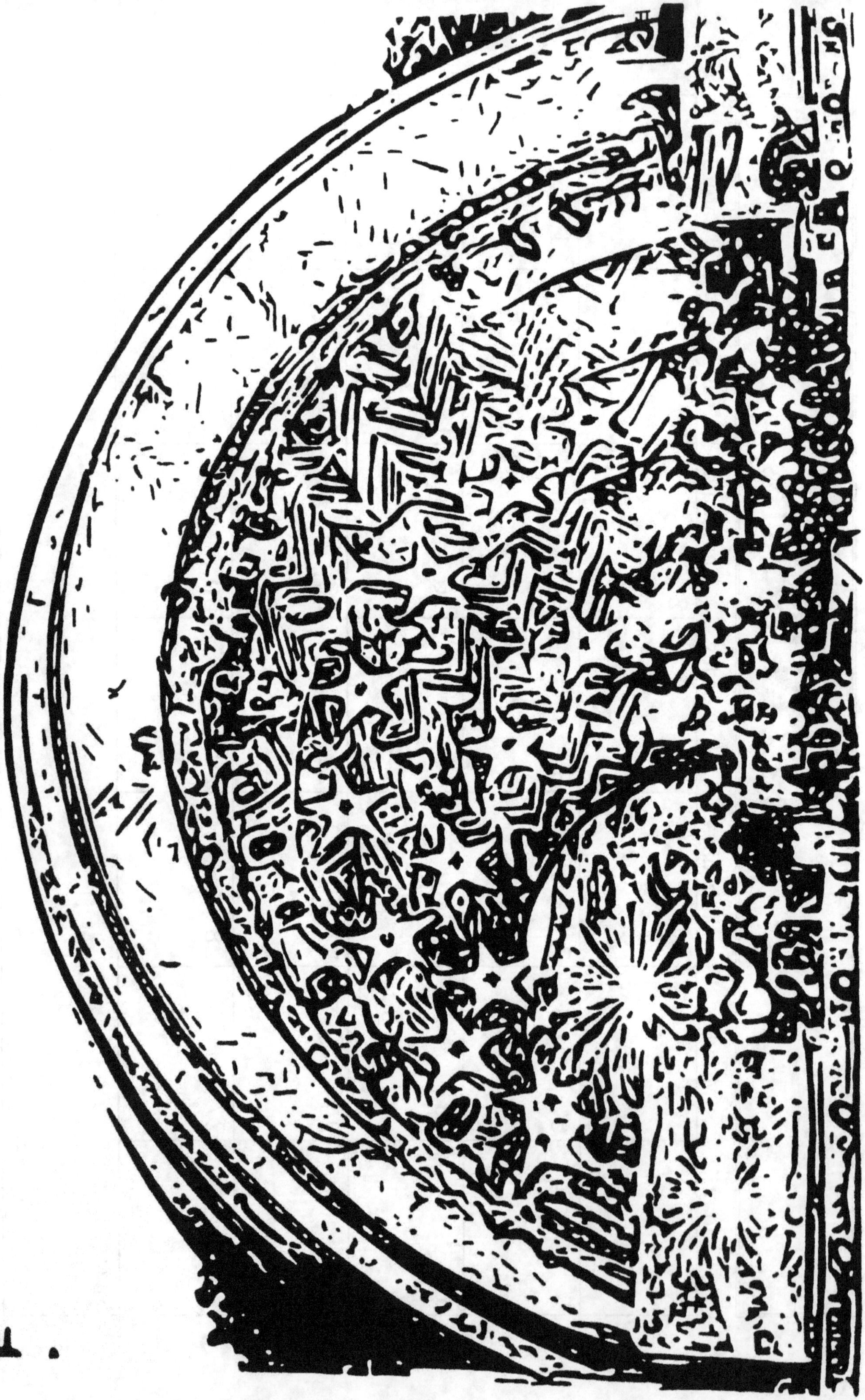

II.

JULY 2016

Sunday	Monday	Tuesday	Wednesday	Thursday	Friday	Saturday
					1	2
3	4	5	6	7	8	9
10	11	12	13	14	15	16
17	18	19	20	21	22	23
24	25	26	27	28	29	30
31	Notes:					

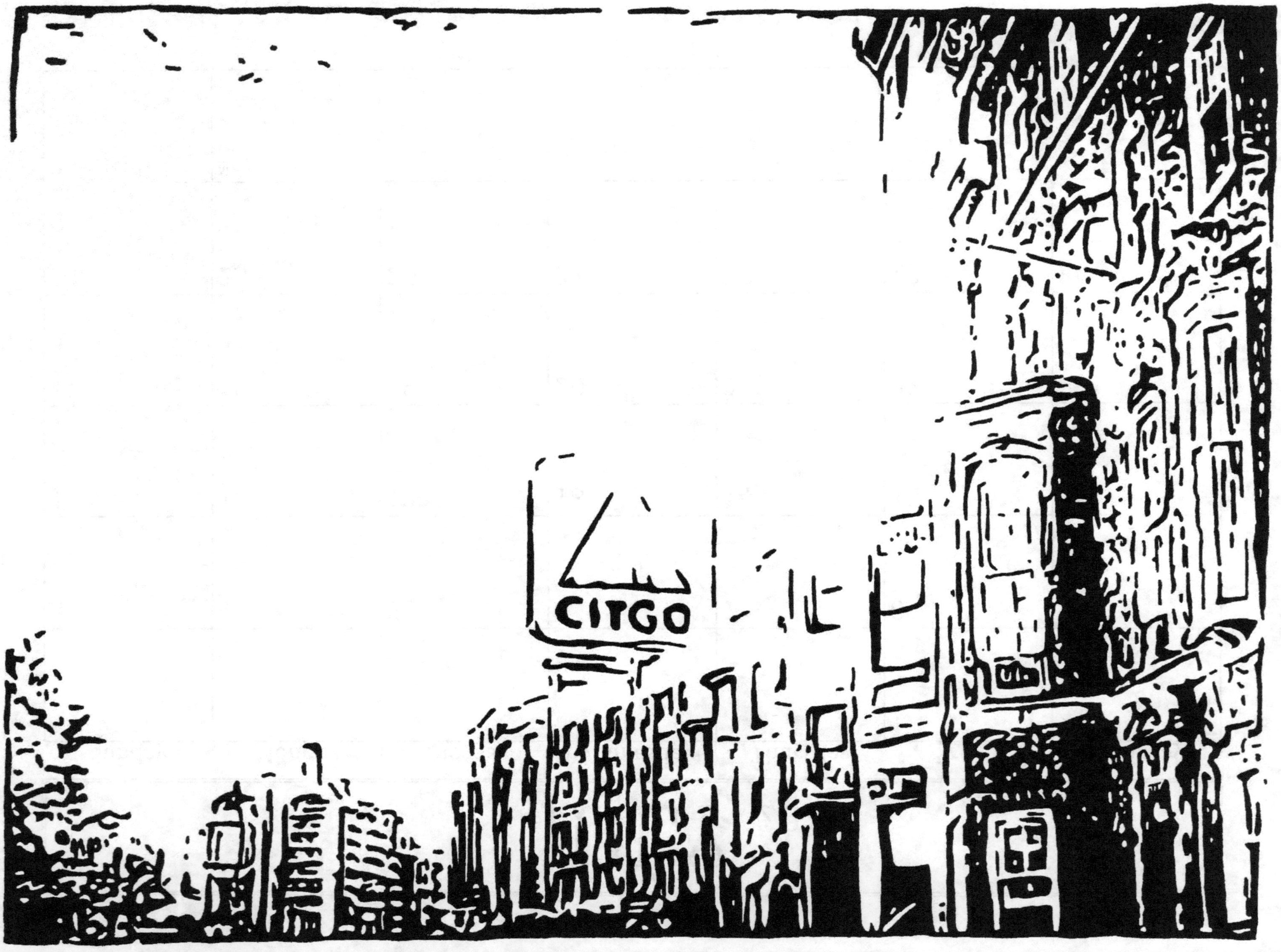
CITGO

AUGUST 2016

Sunday	Monday	Tuesday	Wednesday	Thursday	Friday	Saturday
	1	2	3	4	5	6
7	8	9	10	11	12	13
14	15	16	17	18	19	20
21	22	23	24	25	26	27
28	29	30	31			

Notes:

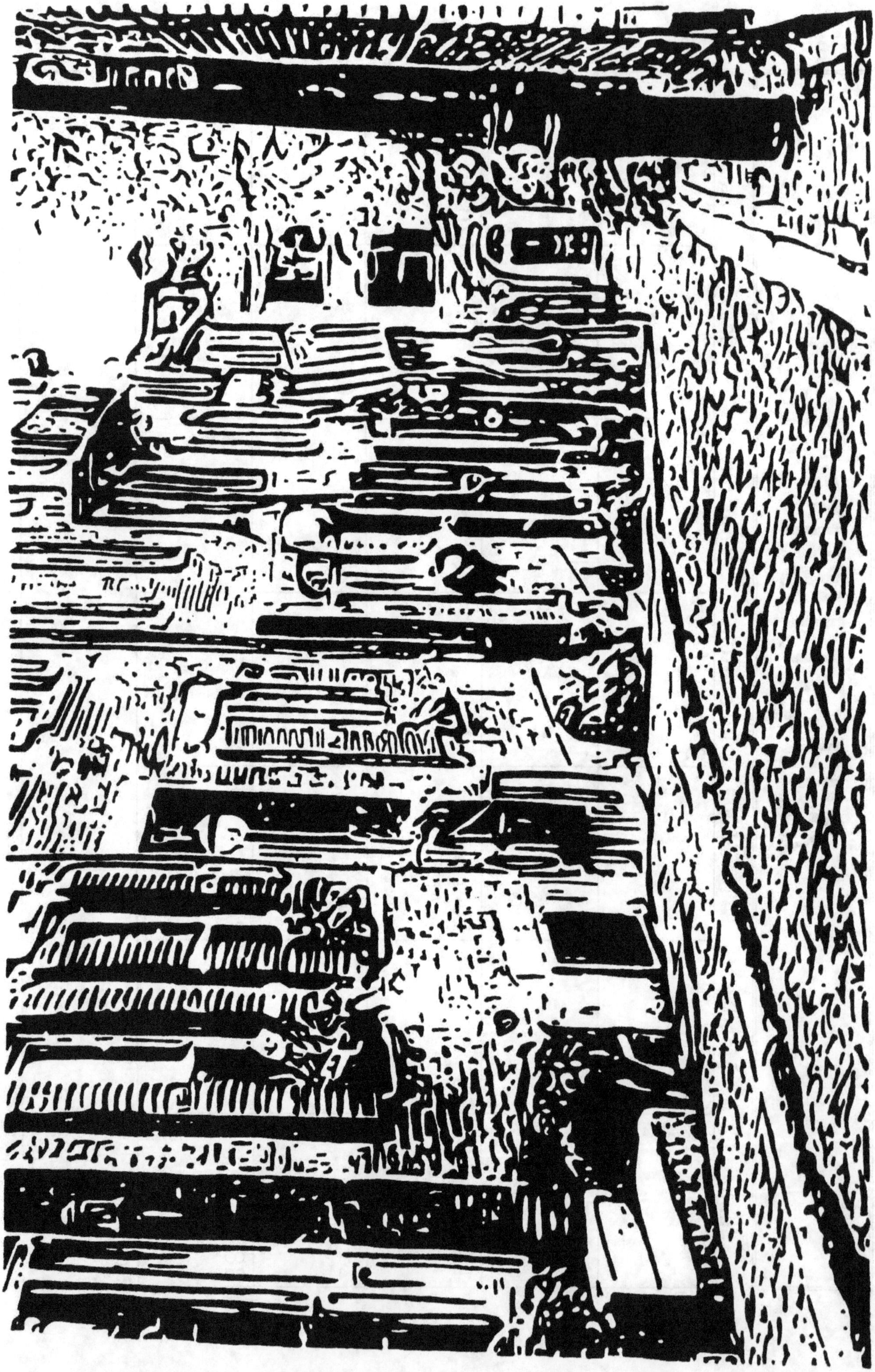

SEPTEMBER 2016

Sunday	Monday	Tuesday	Wednesday	Thursday	Friday	Saturday
				1	2	3
4	5	6	7	8	9	10
11	12	13	14	15	16	17
18	19	20	21	22	23	24
25	26	27	28	29	30	

Notes:

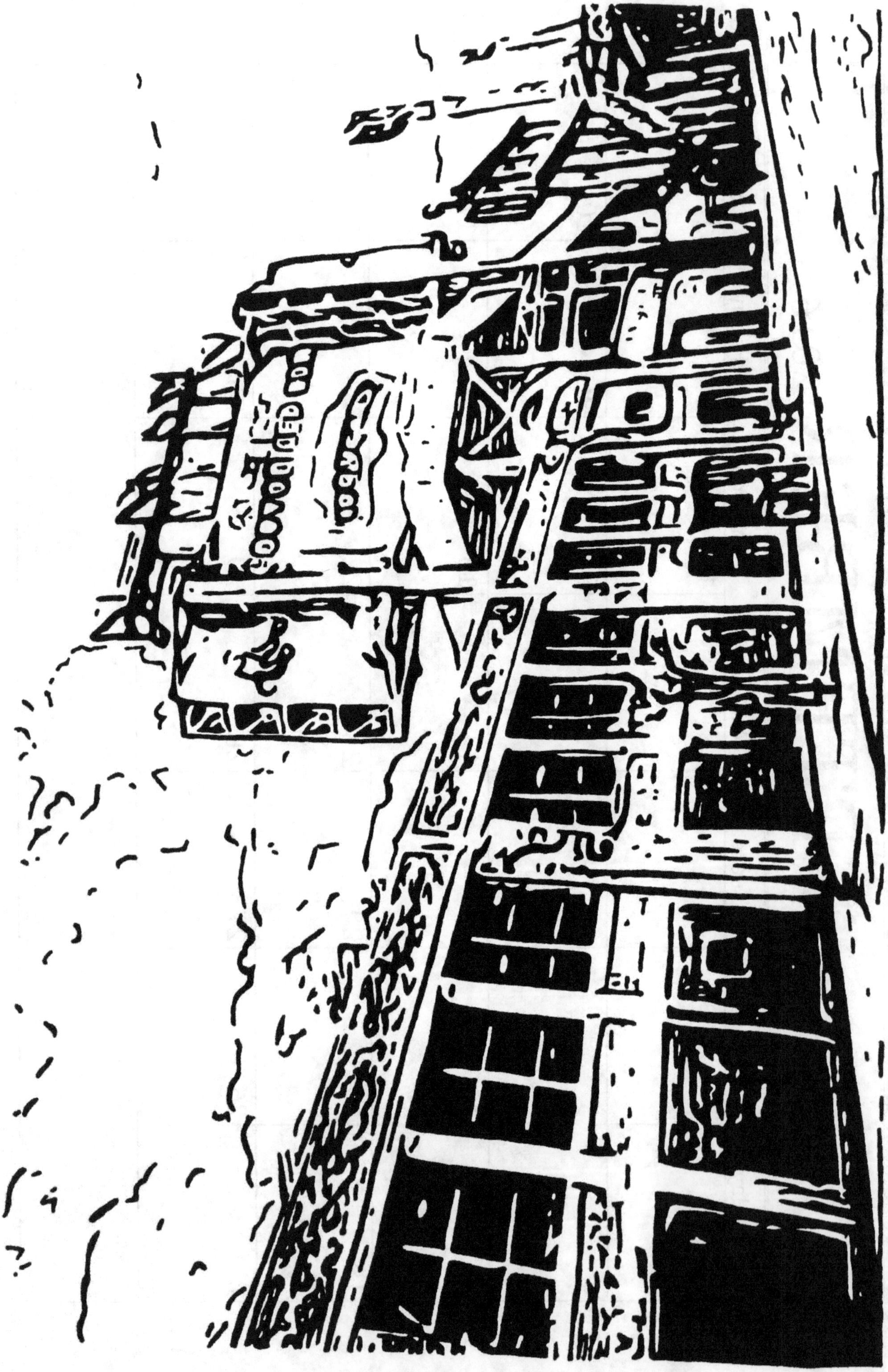

OCTOBER 2016

Sunday	Monday	Tuesday	Wednesday	Thursday	Friday	Saturday
						1
2	3	4	5	6	7	8
9	10	11	12	13	14	15
16	17	18	19	20	21	22
23	24	25	26	27	28	29
30	31	Notes:				

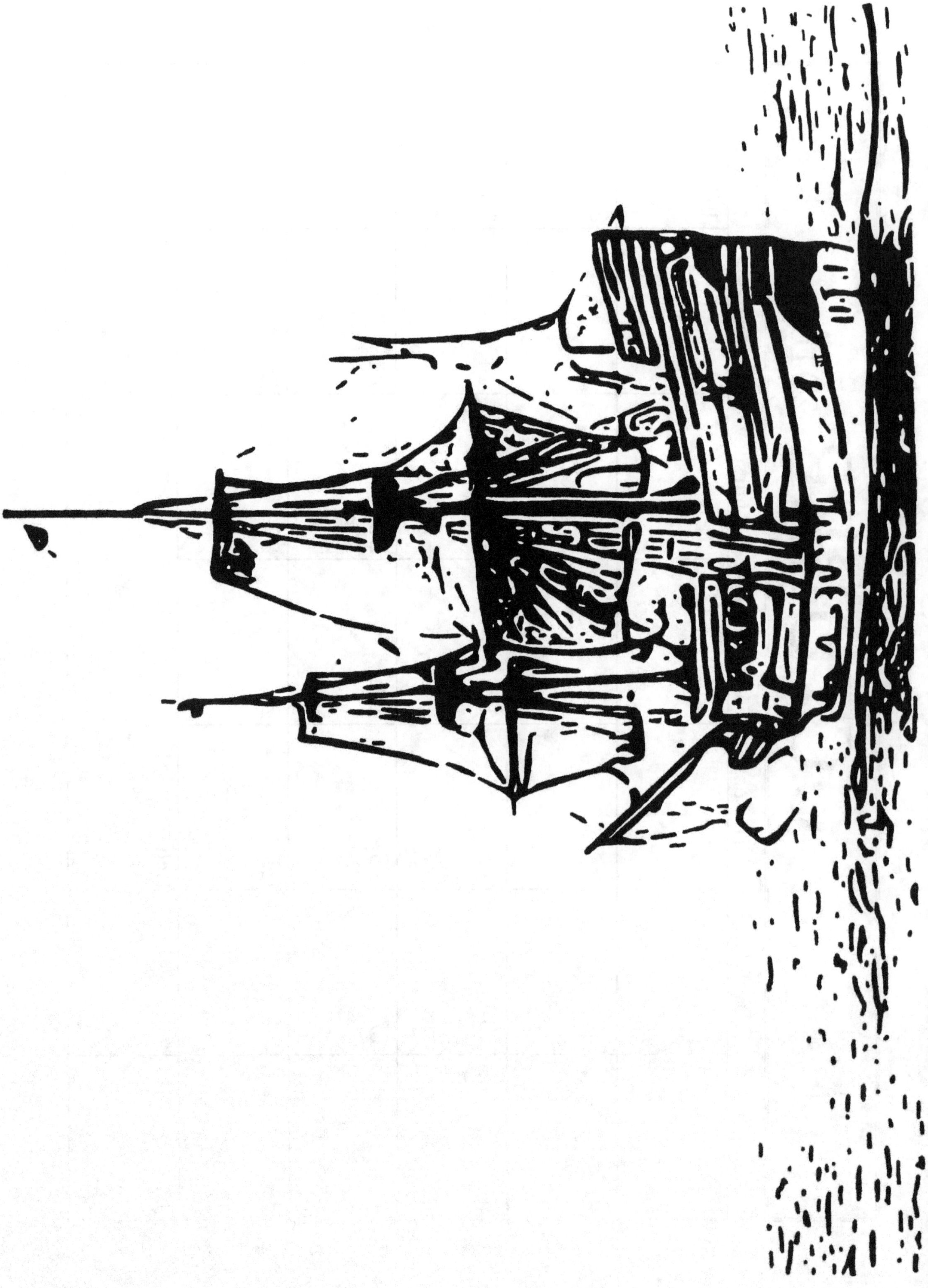

NOVEMBER 2016

Sunday	Monday	Tuesday	Wednesday	Thursday	Friday	Saturday
		1	2	3	4	5
6	7	8	9	10	11	12
13	14	15	16	17	18	19
20	21	22	23	24	25	26
27	28	29	30			

Notes:

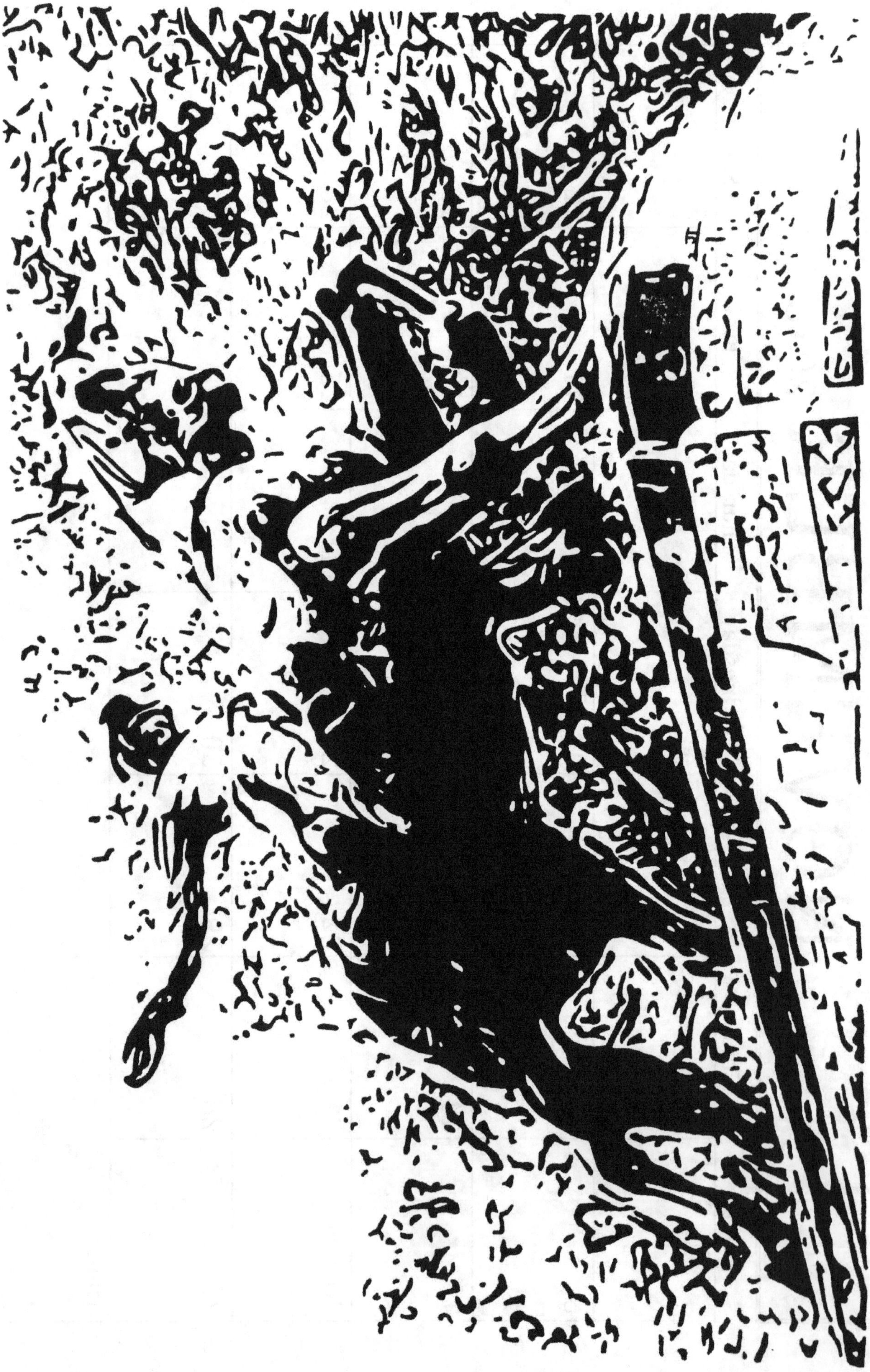

DECEMBER 2016

Sunday	Monday	Tuesday	Wednesday	Thursday	Friday	Saturday
				1	2	3
4	5	6	7	8	9	10
11	12	13	14	15	16	17
18	19	20	21	22	23	24
25	26	27	28	29	30	31

Notes:

www.ingramcontent.com/pod-product-compliance
Lightning Source LLC
Chambersburg PA
CBHW080859170526
45158CB00009B/2780
* 9 7 8 0 6 9 2 5 4 5 2 7 0 *